Defining Moments

SISHMAN RIMPSON

ISBN 979-8-88644-973-0 (Paperback)
ISBN 979-8-88644-975-4 (Hardcover)
ISBN 979-8-88644-974-7 (Digital)

Covenant Books
11661 Hwy 707
Murrells Inlet, SC 29576
www.covenantbooks.com

Contents

Preface..v
Shitty Shitman 1
Living Like a Li'l Man..6
Searching for Identity..11
Time to Man Up...15
Mind Blown..20
An Unexpected U-Turn...31
Digging My Feet in Sacred Soil...35
Feeling Myself...41
A Hard, But Necessary Lesson..46
Hitting Rock Bottom 49
Classes with a Beautiful Lady 54
Realizing It Ain't All About Me...68
A Divine Meeting with "Nate the Great"..............................73
Redeeming Fatherhood 78
A Life-Changing Revelation 87

Preface

"Triplets and twins? Triplets and twins? He has triplets and twins?" The words leaped and sped from table to table as Sishman casually told people about his family at a picnic.

The picnic was hosted by a church group who lived, worked, and shared their lives in the community. Their tone and expressions revealed that everybody knew something was different about Sishman. Only God's favor could provide the same man with a set of triplets and twins.

The culture saw things differently. Having so many children was considered a lack of discipline, or worse, a curse of too many mouths to feed. But God knew what he was doing when he blessed Sishman with those children.

In fact, even though Sishman had six children at that time, God later added to his family, granting this man ten children in his mighty quiver.

Who is this man that has ten children in modern-day times? He is my brother and my friend. Even though his story talks about identity, it reveals a greater question. Who is the God that reveals himself in the defining moments of our lives? Who is the God that allows trying times, but sticks with us in the struggle, pain, and highs and lows of life? This God sees us experience shame, live in sin, fail, labor, and struggle to figure it out, but his love remains. This God, who you'll see all throughout Sishman's story, is a loving Father who redeems all things.

Defining Moments uncovers the reality that an abundant life belongs to those who work diligently and never quit. Throughout their lives, they discover this God. The journey, although difficult at times, is full of personal discovery, love, hope, grace, and understanding. During some of these defining moments, Sishman seemed to fail, but his faith in a loving God promising life more abundantly did not. The God who Sishman finds on this journey of defining moments is faithful. 2 Timothy 2:13 AMP says, "If we are faithless, He remains faithful [true to His word and His righteous character], for He cannot deny Himself." That faithfulness gives us hope for a better tomorrow even on the darkest days.

Sishman's story reminds me of an old hymn called Road to Zion. The words of the song are:

There is a way that leads to life,
The few who find it never die
Past mountain peaks laced white with snow
The way grows brighter as we go

Sometimes a shadow, dark and cold
Falls like a mist across the road
But be encouraged by the sight
Where there's a shadow there's a light

There is a road prepared for you
The destination's sure and true
From pilgrimage do not depart
Run after God with all your heart
Run after God with all your heart

Sometimes it's good to look back down
We've come so far, we've gained such ground
But joy is not in where we've been
Joy is who's waiting at the end
There is a road prepared for you
The destination's sure and true

The Sishman I know has had defining moments along this road. Those moments capture the heart and focus one's attention on destiny, purpose, and an understanding of the continuing love of God that never fails.

During the early days of my friendship with Sishman, I remember us weeping, praying, and rejoicing in the wee hours of the morning. We shared moments of transparent brotherhood as we worked to understand this road together.

Since then, I have watched him grow from a babe in Christ. Now, God uses him to facilitate and teach discipleship principles to others struggling to understand hard moments in their lives.

The defining moments of his life and story have become a bed of seeds revealing the beauty, patience, and long-suffering of God the Father.

Join me as I revisit and return to those moments as we read about the man I am blessed to call a friend.

Earnest Scott

Shitty Shitman

And Nathanael said to him, "Can anything good come
from Nazareth?" Philip said, "Come and see."

—John 1:46

I was born in Gary, Indiana, in an era where, statistically, I didn't
have a shot at success. At the time, Gary was the murder capital of
the nation, and my choices were pretty much picked out for me:
sell drugs, become a hip-hop artist, or engage in criminal activity.
My other two options were to become an athlete or work at the steel
mills.

The city that had a rich history and was once a booming market
for Black people was filled with drugs and violence. Addiction and
street life were the influences that shaped me and plagued my family.

My mom, Karen Harris, was the life of the party. She was loyal,
fun, had a bubbly personality, and a youthful spirit. It seemed like
everyone in Gary knew my mama. They called her "Peaches" back
then. My father, Nate Rimpson, was a gangster, playboy, and certi-
fied hustler. People called him "Nate the Great." My dad had other
kids with other women, a total of five altogether, but in my house
where my mom and three younger sisters lived, I was the man of the
house.

When I was young, my mama told me that I was the man of the
house. That built something in me as a child. So naturally, I became
my mama and sisters' protector. Even though I lived in the murder
capital of the nation, I didn't realize that back then. I was extremely
spoiled by my grandparents, aunts, and uncles. I was named after
my grandfather, and my grandmother pretty much considered me

her baby from birth. I split time between living with my mom and grandma during my early years.

I have several brothers born to women outside of my mom. We all stayed in Gary, Indiana, and didn't know each other existed for years. I remember seeing my dad six times before he went to prison when I was eight years old. But my mother never talked bad about my dad. When she did talk about him, she made him sound like a hero. She said things like, "Boy, your daddy ran from the police today, jumped over cars, dodged bullets, and they still couldn't catch him." I idolized this man, and I'm so grateful to my mama for giving me that.

Unfortunately, in the 1980s, my mom fell victim to drugs. The crack epidemic was strong in ghettos across the United States. Our quality of life started to decline as my mom got caught up in that lifestyle. As the years passed her addiction grew stronger, and we eventually hit rock bottom. It was no secret my mom abused drugs, and some of the kids in the projects could be cruel. Even though my mom was on drugs, I felt like I had to protect her name and my sisters from the bullying. On top of all that, I had to be the man of the house.

Things got really bad during that time. I began to steal food from local stores and would sometimes borrow hot dogs from neighbors. Although it wasn't an everyday occurrence, there were times I had to step in and take care of things. But I couldn't take care of everything—like how poor we were.

I remember on one occasion stealing shoes from a Salvation Army dumpster. I climbed into the dumpster and found a pair of Reeboks. They were old, stinking, beat-up shoes, but they had the name Reebok on them. They were like three sizes bigger than my feet, so the neighborhood kids called me Bozo. It was tough, but my sisters and I got extremely close during those times. We made the best out of what we had.

I was the oldest of my mom's kids, so I willfully took on the brunt of the verbal attacks from cruel kids in the neighborhood. I usually was able to take the attacks and keep it moving, but I remember one time I almost broke down. The kids at my school nicknamed me "Shitty Shitman." I hated that nickname with a passion. I was only eleven years old at the time, and my sisters were nine, eight, and six. We didn't wash our clothes often. Sometimes we wore the same socks for weeks. We didn't have toothpaste to brush our teeth. We used baking soda. We didn't have lotion, so we used lard. We didn't have an iron, so we would heat a frying pan and put our clothes underneath the bottom of it. So imagine smelling like a hot frying pan, Crisco grease, and stinking clothes that hadn't been washed for weeks. We smelled horrible, and the neighborhood kids were sure to let us know.

I didn't fight for my name, but I got protective when people talked about my sisters. There were definitely some days when I fought back tears. Imagine sitting on the bus and everyone laughing at your new oversized Reeboks and your new nickname, "Shitty Shitman."

I remember the kids walking by, pointing, and laughing at my shoes. It was humbling, but it was a defining moment for me. I remember thinking to myself back then with a tear running down my face, *this isn't going to be my life forever*. I told myself that day, "One of these days, I'll be able to buy me some Jordans."

I was right. That wasn't my life forever, and God has blessed me to acquire plenty of brand-name stuff to make up for what little Sishman didn't have back then. Growing up in those surroundings could make you ask, "Can anything good come from the hood?" But even at a young age, I made up my mind that I was going to beat the odds. Shitty Shitman is a part of my story. I laugh now when I tell it to my children and to young adults I mentor. Only God can take what once caused so much pain and confusion and use it as a tool to motivate a young Sishman and inspire countless others.

Me and my precious grandmother, (Mothers). She helped raise
me the majority of my life growing up. Love and miss her so!

On a visit home from Texas to visit my Mothers. She was so
excited to see me whenever I came home from Texas.

Living Like a Li'l Man

Be watchful…act like men, be strong.
Let all you do be done in love.

—1 Corinthians 16:13–14

I always say, *a made-up mind is undefeated,* but just because I made up my mind to beat the odds doesn't mean life got easier. After one of my uncles died, we moved to Rock Island, Illinois. In many ways, the name was symbolic because that was the place where we really hit rock bottom. At first, things were going good. My mom was really trying to beat her addiction. She was open with her children about her struggles, and we all were rooting for our mama. She really tried to make a change. But eventually, she started finding friends who were similar to the people she hung out with back home. She became really cool with Charles, one of our neighbors in the apartment we lived in. But Charles was on drugs and reintroduced my mom to that lifestyle.

It wasn't long before my mom was back using heavy. We lost the apartment and moved around a lot and eventually ended up in a semi-complete rental home my sisters and I called, "The Brown House." As luck would have it, the neighbors across the street were drug users and dealers. Living that close to drug dealers led my mom on a downward spiral. We eventually lost the brown house as well. We put all of our clothes in a plastic bag and walked a few miles to Arsenal Courts Housing Projects, our new home and rock bottom for my mom and her children. Since we had moved away from Gary, there was no one around to hold my mom accountable. I was a teenager during these years and took advantage of having a lack of supervision. My friends and I started to emulate what we saw the dope boys doing.

I watched and studied when drug dealers would cook rocks over one of my friend's, whose brother was a dealer, houses. I can still remember the smell of cocaine being cooked into rocks. Even though I was a kid, I learned how to make baking soda look like crack cocaine. I'm not proud of it, but when we needed money or I wanted something, I would mislead people struggling with addiction and sell them a fake rock for $20. By the time they figured it out, I was gone. Yes, I was a hustler even as a teenager.

At first, I used that freedom to stay out until three or four o'clock in the morning. But eventually, I got a job. My job was to carry one of the hood dope dealers' money in a plastic bag to another home he operated out of in our projects. He paid me $20 per trip! One day he left the window down in his van. When he got out of the vehicle and went into the local candy store, he had thousands of dollars unsecured in his car. A strong wind came through and blew stacks of his money out the window and into the streets. There were $20 bills everywhere. I grabbed about $200 and my sisters grabbed about $300. Fred, the drug dealer I worked for, was pissed. He came banging on our door, looking for his money. I was so scared for my mom, but she stood her ground and told him, "I don't know what you're talking about." I was afraid he was going to shoot my mom, but after a while, he believed her and let it go.

Life was tough in Arsenal Courts Projects, but I met one of my closest friends during that time. His name is James Rogers. James was a little bit younger than me and was like my little brother. His parents loved me and took me in. Even though we lived in the projects together, his mom and dad had set a foundation for him that was so different.

I would look at his life and long for the foundation, structure, and family dynamics he had. Part envious and part inspired, I pushed myself onto the Rogers family because I wanted that feeling of a close-knit family for myself. His mom wasn't on drugs. She worked. His dad was a chef. They could've easily pushed me away. I was this smelly kid who was about three years older than their son. But they let me in. Spending time with that family was therapeutic for me.

I was trying to be the li'l man everyone needed, wanted, and expected me to be, but at James's house, I saw a different perspective of what it meant to be a man.

Even though I was doing the wrong thing, I was trying to do the right thing.

I stole food because I was hungry and I needed to eat, but I knew there was a better way. Although I wasn't going to church often, the conviction never left me when doing wrong.

I sold people fake drugs because my family needed the money, but I didn't want to hurt people to take care of the people I loved.

I worked for a drug dealer because I wanted to provide for my mom and sisters, but I needed a better job. I wanted the kind of job James's parents had.

The little man I had become wasn't the man I longed to be. Nothing about my life changed overnight, and as I got older, I started to think about who I really wanted to become.

I wanted to be the kind of man my mom and sisters could rely on. But the reality was that I was a young man trying to figure myself and my life out under a lot of pressure.

My mom and her four children. This was during the time my
mom was trying to break her addiction in the early 90s.

My grandmother and my Aunties (Big Sisters). I ADORE
my aunties! I'm still their lil'man to this day!

Me and my Uncles Jesse, Melvin, and Reggie! I love these men with all my heart! I had many fathers growing up!

Searching for Identity

But as for you, O Man of God, flee these things. Pursue righteousness, godliness, faith, love, steadfastness, and gentleness.

—1 Timothy 6:11

While I tried to figure out whom I wanted to be, life experiences showed me what I didn't want to be.

I was in fourth grade when my mom got shot. That made me realize I didn't want to be a gun person.

It was a scary night at 2962 West 11th Avenue, our apartment right next door to Gary, Indiana, royalty, the Brookshire family. My sisters and I were used to lying in the bed by ourselves. But when we woke up, my auntie Cat was sitting in the bed with us, which never happens. She's one of my mom's younger sisters. My sisters and I asked, "What's going on?" That's when my aunt told us my mom got shot.

She said the bullet went into the top of her head and came right back out.

I remember hearing gunshots that night, but that was a normal occurrence. It was nothing out of the ordinary. But knowing what happened scared us. We didn't want to be there. We didn't know if whoever did it was going to come back to the house. So we went with my auntie Cat back to my grandmother's house.

My mom never told us who shot her. It's rumored that it was one of our cousins, that they were arguing over drugs. Others think that it was my two younger sisters' dad. We never really knew the details, but we always felt like it was over drugs. I respect my mom's decision to keep that private. Whoever it was, she didn't want us to know. I'm just glad my mom survived.

Seeing my dad go to prison made me realize I didn't want to be a gangster and end up in jail.

Even though I had only seen my dad about six times since I was born, I knew he was into the street life and pimping. When I was about eight or nine years old, that lifestyle caught up to him. I don't know all the details, but something went wrong, and my dad and one of his partners killed two people. After running from the police for a year, my dad decided to turn himself in. I didn't know it at the time, but he was coming to say goodbye.

I was outside playing at 2962 West 11th Avenue, and I saw this guy out of the corner of my eye walking up toward me with a three-piece white suit on. My daddy wore suits everywhere and this man had the same walk my daddy did. I glanced back at this man and said, "Daddy?"

He said, "Come here, boy," and I ran and jumped into my daddy's arms. He came upstairs, hugged my mom, and he stayed with us for about an hour.

And then he said, "L'il man, come ride with me." So I rode with him on his farewell tour, unbeknownst to me. We stopped at a home in Ivanhoe Projects, and my dad went inside for a long time. When he came out this little boy was with him, and he was crying so hard. I couldn't figure out why he was crying so much, but his name was Nate, just like my daddy.

Trying to figure out who he was, I asked his last name. "Nate what?"

He said, "Nate Rimpson." That was the day I found out I had a brother. He was about three or four years older than me, but it blew my mind that I had a brother all this time.

My dad stayed at that place for a while. Young Nate was so heartbroken. I didn't understand it. All I knew was that I got to see my daddy. It had been two years since I last saw him. I was so excited because I didn't know the next time I would see him, and I clearly didn't understand that he was going away, but my brother was crying so hard.

Next, my dad went to see my grandma who was at my Aunt Michelle's house at the time. Another one of my aunts was married to a Gary police officer. My dad rang the doorbell, and when my grandmother answered it, he said, "Mama, if Larry's up there with the police, I don't want to have to kill anybody." My grandmother assured him that my Uncle Larry, nor the GPD were at my aunties home.

My dad went upstairs, said his goodbyes to them and lastly to me, and left me there. I didn't see my dad again after that day for twenty-one years.

Growing up during the crack epidemic of the 1980s has caused a great deal of post-traumatic stress disorder in many of us born and raised in that era. I remember watching women in the projects battling addiction do unseemly things for the next hit. I would turn a corner and see things I shouldn't have as a child. I remember on a particular occasion, I saw my older cousin Melton sell my mom, his auntie drugs. "Mel Mel," as he was known by our family, was a cousin I looked up to at one point in my life. I couldn't understand how he could sell his own auntie the drugs that were destroying her and our family. One day, some years later, I gathered the courage to confront him. I was in high school at the time, and even though I wasn't the type of person to keep hatred in my heart, I was angry and confused.

We were playing video games at my uncle Melvin's house, but the question was just burning inside me. "Mel," I said, interrupting the game.

"What's up L'il Man?" he responded.

"How could you sell drugs to your auntie and my mama?" I'll never forget the look on his face.

"Lil cuz," he said, "I feel like if you could whoop me right now, you would." Then he said, "Cuz, I know this may not sound right, but I would rather auntie Peaches get it from me than get it from somebody else." At the time, I thought that was the lamest excuse I'd ever heard, but in his jacked-up mind, that was his way of caring for her. He actually believed what he said.

It was an eye-opening moment. It brought to mind what Jay Z meant in one of his songs when he said, you can be addicted to crack in more ways than one. Those addicted to using it and those addicted to the fast money it brings selling it.

I'm not pointing the finger at my cousin or anybody else. That conversation made me realize I would never sell crack. These defining moments in my life gave me these markers that I wasn't going to cross.

Experiencing these moments at a young age was tough, but I never looked at the glass as half empty. I always say the glass is half full.

My dad's absence taught me that I was going to be there for my children.

My mom being strung out on drugs taught me not to touch drugs.

I realized that when I made up my mind about something, it got done. I didn't know that was a strength. But it stopped me from making excuses and feeling like a victim.

Life dealt me some ugly blows, but I used them as life lessons. I learned whom I did and didn't want to be. I learned what I did and didn't want to do. I learned about places I never wanted to go. And I've carried those lessons with me all throughout my life.

Time to Man Up

When I was a child, I spoke as a child, I understood
as a child, I thought as a child, but when I became
a man, I put away childish things.

—1 Corinthians 13:11

On February 16, 2001, the entire trajectory of my life changed. My daughter, Ameia Rimpson, was born, and her birth forced me to make the first grown-up decision I ever made in my life.

Even though I was working at the time, I was only making $6 an hour. I could barely afford Pampers for my baby. I knew something had to change. I just couldn't fathom not being able to take care of my child. The thought of that made me cringe and messed with my entire being. As I was looking for a better job, I saw an ad in the paper. When I went to the place listed in the paper, I realized that the advertisement was created by a military recruiter for the Marines. I was so desperate to provide for my child, I went and took the test the next day.

I scored an eighty-six on the Armed Service Vocational Aptitude Battery (ASVAB) test which was crazy. I tried to take the same test three times when I graduated from high school, and I couldn't score high enough to get accepted into any of the branches of the military. But on that day, I was taking the test for Ameia and I scored an eighty-six on that bad boy. When I realized I could get into the Air Force with that score, I left the Marine recruiter's office and walked over to the Air Force Recruiters office. A week and a half later, I left for boot camp at Lackland Air Force Base in San Antonio, Texas. That was the first grown-man decision I'd made in my life.

Ameia was three months old, and I knew I had to take care of my daughter by any means necessary. If that meant I had to leave everything, I had to leave everything: Gary, the Quad Cities, my girlfriend, my grandma. My mother. My sisters. My aunties. My friends. I left it all for Ameia. I wanted and had to do better for her. So I joined the Air Force, got on a plane for the first time, and headed to boot camp in San Antonio.

I arrived at Lackland AFB on May 22, 2001. When I got off the bus that took us to the base from the airport, the training instructor screamed at me. I accidentally touched the rail, and he said, "Touch that rail again and I'll break my foot off in your you know what." It was a culture shock. Up until that moment, I was a young man who didn't have any structure or discipline. I hadn't even stayed on a job longer than six months. As the yelling and screaming continued, I asked myself what in the world did I get myself into.

Most of the guys in the squadron were young and focused on physicality. I quickly learned to be slow to speak and ready to listen. Attention to detail was key to being successful in boot camp. Thanks to that mindset, I quickly became a leader in our group. I was chosen to lead because I was older and I loved drill. I was selected to be the guidon bearer for our squadron. That meant I had to carry the flag and lead the entire flight of fifty-two airmen. If I went right, the entire flight went right. If I did something wrong, the entire flight did something wrong. The pressure was on me. It was my first leadership role, and I didn't have a lot of confidence.

Up until my joining the Air Force, the consistent authoritative figures in my life were women. I did have my uncles Reggie and Melvin, but they weren't as consistent in my formative years as my grandmother, aunties, and teachers growing up.

I didn't have a man in my life who consistently showed me how to be a man. My dad was in prison. My uncle Reggie was an insurance man, so he worked all the time. I had no man at home growing up, so my confidence was shot. I lacked the confidence my peers exhibited while in boot camp.

In many ways, God changed my life through the military and gave me the discipline I never knew existed as a young man growing up in the hood. I learned how to follow.

In the military, following is a form of leadership because when you do what's right and you listen, those in your sphere of influence are going to follow your lead.

After basic training, Ameia's mother and my uncle Reggie came up for my graduation. They were shocked when they saw me because I was so different. I wasn't a li'l man running the streets trying to figure things out anymore. I was disciplined. My stature was upright, I stood taller, and I had confidence! I stood up straight and tall. Everything about me had changed in that small amount of time.

The impact the military had on my life and who I was as a man wasn't a temporary impression, but a permanent impact. I still live by the Air Force's core values: service before self, integrity first, and excellence in everything you do. They instilled those core values in me during the first six weeks of boot camp. But little did I know that those core values would take me far beyond my six years in the Air Force. Those were the values that shaped my new life.

I left Gary, Indiana, and the Midwest as a whole and I have never returned. Here I am twenty-one years later, and I'm still in San Antonio, Texas.

Life was on the up and up. I was able to buy Pampers for my daughter now. I had put away childish things and become a man. I felt this incredible sense of accomplishment in everything I'd become as an airman and was able to accomplish.

All of it was for my baby girl, Ameia. She changed my life in more ways than one.

My graduation from Air Force Basic Training, holding my
6-month-old daughter, Ameia. She changed my life forever.

A young Airman Rimpson at the 651st Munitions Squadron.
My first and only duty station during my Air Force career.

Mind Blown

Now all glory to God, who is able, through his
mighty power at work within us, to accomplish
infinitely more than we can ask or think.

—Ephesians 3:20

After boot camp, I went to tech school. It was a training center where I learned how to do my job in the Air Force. Even though it was like a college environment that required me to stay indoors and learn, it was the most fun time I ever had in my life.

I was an ammunition specialist. I learned about missiles and bombs. I finally felt a level of competency in something, which was such an accomplishment for me because I hated school. But at the time I felt so proud because I was actually learning something, and it was fun. I was doing something special.

I started tech school in August 2001, and everything was great up until September. On September 11, 2001, the world changed, especially America as we knew it. The Twin Towers were attacked by a terrorist. My career, which had up until that point been fun and games, became very serious. They called us to the auditorium and told us, "The United States is at war." Everything changed in that moment.

Before September 11, you could get on the base by simply showing your driver's license. After the attack, the level of alert was so high that now you can't get onto a military base unless you have a military ID. Everything in the Air Force changed. Things became serious. No more laughing. No more joking. I started to experience a level of pride in my country that I didn't have before. I mean, a terrorist attacked us and killed more than five thousand Americans. Even though I was from the hood, the people that I was serving with all had a common denominator. Despite our differences, we all joined together in service to our country during September 11, 2001. My peers and I started to experience a level of pride in our work that we didn't have before. After finishing tech school, it was time for us to get our orders.

Some people got orders to go to Florida and other places around the world. I got orders to go to Aviano Air Force base in Italy. As exciting as that was, all I could think about was leaving my six-month-old daughter. I couldn't function thinking about leaving my baby. I loved Ameia more than anything else on earth. I pulled one of my sergeants aside and said, "Man, I'm having some anxiety about my orders." He gave me some great and wise advice.

He said, "Not too many people know this, but if you are married as a first-time airman, they can't send you overseas." So I called my girlfriend at the time and was like, "Let's do this. Let's get married. It wasn't a romantic proposal or anything, and we definitely weren't ready for marriage, but we knew what we had to do."

I didn't want to go overseas, and she didn't want me to go overseas because she didn't want to raise Ameia by herself. So I said, "Let's do it."

She was like, "Let's go." We didn't involve our parents. We didn't do anything formal or fancy. She came down to Wichita Falls which was where the tech school was, and we went to the courthouse. We did the best thing we thought we should do at that time. I got my paperwork saying I was married, she got back on the plane and went home, and I continued to live my life. Even though I was married, nothing about my mindset changed.

I turned my certificate of marriage in and they changed my orders. Instead of Italy, my orders were to Lackland Air Force Base in San Antonio, Texas, where I was during boot camp. So I got sent back to Lackland, but there's an annex there called Medina and that's where I was stationed. After graduating from tech school, the Air Force allows you to go home for two weeks to get your family if you're married. So I went home and asked her, "Are you going to come to Texas with me?"

She said, "Well, we're married."

So we packed up all her stuff, got Ameia, and within two weeks, we were on a plane headed to our new home in San Antonio. Everything happened so fast.

When I got back on base, because of September 11, everyone was working twelve hours, seven days a week. For the next thirty-six days, I worked twelve hours a day, seven days a week, shipping out bombs. It was insane.

Ameia's mother was by herself a lot because I was working so much. She had to deal with the baby and military life all at once. My first supervisor in the military was Tech Sergeant Dell Jennis. He was the guy who showed me the ropes. He wouldn't let anybody touch me. I was his little brother in our military family. I got away with a lot of stuff which caused a lot of my peers to be jealous. Most of the older Black sergeants in my squadron looked out for me. There were only about seven of them in a squadron of one hundred thirty people. But the brothers took me under their wing and showed me the good and bad about military life. They exposed me to a lot.

About a year after arriving to Lackland, I found out that my wife was pregnant. Even though I was in the military now, I was scared. I was only making $900 a month. How was I going to make enough for two kids? I was only an E-3 in the military. But eventually, I calmed down. I was like this is perfect. I have a daughter. Hopefully, this baby will be a son.

When my wife at the time was four months pregnant, I noticed that she had put on a lot of weight during this new pregnancy. I never said anything. I just figured we'd have a chunky baby.

One day we decided to go out to get something to eat, and somebody hit the car and rear-ended us. We were both scared. We drove to Wilford Hall, the military hospital in San Antonio. The doctor decided to do an ultrasound to make sure the baby was good. After examining us further, the ER doctor decided to send us upstairs to the maternity ward for a more detailed ultrasound. He was concerned because the babies' heartbeat was beating faster than normal.

We were so nervous. I remember thinking, *God, please don't take my son.* We didn't even know the gender of the baby, but I was already claiming a son. So we went upstairs. They were doing the detailed ultrasound. I could never really read or understand those things. I'll never forget: the doctor dropped his jaw while looking at the ultrasound screen.

I said, "Doctor, what's wrong? Just tell us what's going on."

"Oh, no, no no, Mr. Rimpson," he replied. "No, no, no, please come here," he asked.

"What is going on?" I was completely anxious at this point.

He said, "Everything is fine."

"Why do you have that shocked look on your face then?"

He said, "I'm going to show you. Are you ready?"

"Yes."

"There's baby A," he said, showing me the heartbeat. "There's baby B," he said, showing me a second heartbeat, "And there's baby C," he said, showing me the third heartbeat.

"I'm confused. What do you mean?"

He said, "Sir, your wife is pregnant with triplets."

I started hyperventilating instantly. My wife started screaming. I had asthma, so they had to hook me up to a breathing machine. The doctor was laughing because he couldn't believe I was actually having an asthma attack. Talk about a defining moment! We had just found out that we were about to go from one child to four with $900 a month in income from the military.

We rode home from the hospital in complete and utter silence. I went and told one of my other sergeants about everything. He meant well, but he didn't give me good advice. He said, "Sishman, you gotta have an abortion." Of course, he was looking at the fact that I was only making $900. He said, "You cannot do this."

Sergeant Jennis, hearing what he said to me, let me know that he would never tell me to get an abortion, but that this was going to be tough. So I started thinking about how I was going to make this happen. I was scared. I had never thought about abortion in my life. But I kept thinking to myself, *how am I going to raise four kids with $900 a month?* It was a month of pure anxiety. I was a walking zombie. I drowned myself in work. Every time they needed somebody to work extra, I volunteered. We were extremely stressed. It was just a crazy time for us. Our marriage took a backseat to being parents.

I didn't know how we were going to do it, but I made up my mind that we weren't going to have an abortion.

My mind was blown, yes! But it was also made up. I was determined to find a way to make it work. I eventually learned one of the greatest truths ever, and that's that "a made-up mind is undefeated."

My sons, the triplets! My greatest inspiration to become successful. I just wanted to be a positive example to my sons.

The relationship I have with my sons is unbreakable! There has never been a lack of love or affection between us.

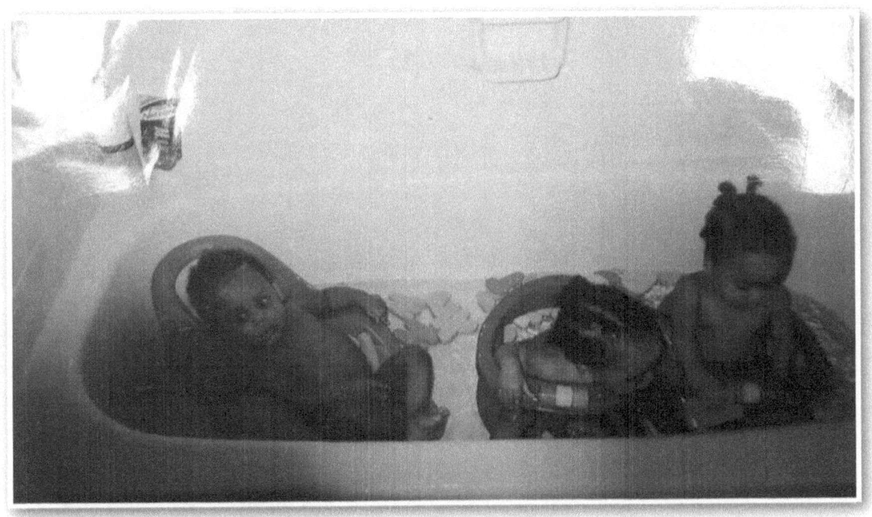

I believe this was after one of their many accidents! It was definitely a stinky situation, and a bath was warranted!

Love this pic. It shows all of their personalities. Especially
Antonio's with his sinister smile in the middle.

Me and my baby girls! Ameia and the twins, Alicia and Naomi.

Six kids in three years! What were the odds!! Single, triplets, and twins!

An Unexpected U-Turn

But now, this is what the Lord says—He who created you,
Jacob, He who formed you, Israel: "Do not fear, for I have
redeemed you. I have summoned you by name; You are mine."

—Isaiah 43:1

As the pregnancy progressed, we found out the sex of the trip-lets were all boys! Wow! I'm having three sons at the same time! Yes, boys! Finding that out was one of the happiest moments of my life. Every fear and doubt that I had was gone. I felt amazing finding out about all of my children, but when I found out I was having three boys with my last name, I was the happiest dude on earth. I actually got mad at the people who suggested we have an abortion. I was just so ecstatic and motivated to be a good father.

At around twenty weeks into the pregnancy, my wife began to have issues. Full-term for triplets is usually around thirty-two weeks. The doctors were afraid she'd have to go on bed rest for the last two months of the pregnancy so that the babies could continue to develop. We had no family in San Antonio to help us, so the Air Force allowed us to return back to the Midwest, where our families were, to have the babies there.

The Air Force assigned me to the recruiters' office there until the babies were healthy enough to travel. That was the biggest blessing in the world to me because they showed care for me and my family during a time of war. That showed me how much the Air Force valued family. The Air Force did way more for me during the six years I served than I did for it.

When we returned back to the Midwest, our doctor was Dr. John Leno. He was Ameia's doctor also and he coached us through the birth of the triplets. The local newspaper actually came and did a report on us at Dr. Leno's office. The boys were born on July 30, 2002.

I'll never forget how the triplets were born from a C-section. When they pulled the boys out, they were so used to being entangled in the womb that their fingers and limbs were still tangled up. It was crazy. They pulled the long light-skinned baby out first. That's who I named Sishman Jr. Then they pulled a chocolate dark-skinned little baby out. We named him Antonio. The last triplet had chubby jaws. He was the baby of the triplets, and we named him Jalen. The doctors had kind of prepped us to lose the middle triplet because his heart rate was so low throughout the pregnancy, but gratefully, Antonio lived. Their birth was one of the greatest defining moments of my life.

The motivation to provide for them hit me hard. I didn't know what I was going to do, but I was determined to take care of my family. I felt that hustler spirit rise up in me. I'm talking about a hustling mentality. I just kept thinking to myself, *Sishman, you have four kids. It's time to rise up.*

We actually stayed in Illinois for six more weeks. They kept the triplets in the hospital for four weeks, and we stayed with my in-laws for another two weeks. Then we rented a van, packed everyone up, and drove eighteen hours back to San Antonio.

Thanks to that hustler mode, I found out there was an allowance I could get since my family was so large and my base pay was so small. It was called the family subsistence allowance, and it was like the military's equivalent to food stamps. My sergeants approved it, and that brought in an extra $600 a month. I also went off base and applied for food stamps. I began to figure out ways to take care of my family.

My commander Major Brooks had also tasked the squadron to help me out. So my Air Force squadron purchased cribs for all of our babies. They also purchased all of the car seats we needed, but we didn't have a car big enough to fit everyone.

One Saturday, Major Brooks asked my wife and I to meet her at the commissary. "Bring the kids too," she said. My wife and I were like *oh goodness, what's happening?* When we arrived at the commissary, Major Brooks was there with her husband and son. She said, "My family and I just wanted to meet you because we have something for you. We just want you to sign this," she said, handing me this paper that said title for $1. "Do you have a dollar?"

"I think I got some change," I said, grabbing some change out of my car. Her husband pulled up in another car.

"Okay, $1 it is," she said, before continuing to say, "Here are the keys to your new van." She gave my family her family's van for $1.

It hard for me now to not see the hand of God. Without going to church or anything at that time, I started to feel the presence of God hovering over my family through miracles like this one.

I was still living the military life when my sons were born. I was clubbing and hanging out with my friends. My marriage suffered at that time. I was still immature, and we really didn't have any time to connect or do anything together because the triplets were all on different sleeping schedules. It was crazy. One would wake up at 2:00 a.m. in the morning. Another woke up at 4:00 a.m. in the morning. And the other would wake up at 7:00 a.m.

Things were extremely stressful for my wife because I was still in the military, and Uncle Sam controlled my life and my time. She was at home all the time with four babies. I'll never forget: I went out drinking with friends on September 6, 2003. While I was at the bar, I couldn't help but think to myself, *why am I here?*

It was two in the morning, and my wife was home with the kids while I was out at a bar. I was just like *what type of man am I?* So I went home. I looked at my sons. They were asleep. I looked at my wife and Ameia. They were also asleep. I knew I wasn't being a good example or leader for any of them. I don't know why but at that moment, I felt an urge to look up local pastors and churches in the area.

My family back home always tried to get me to go to a certain type of church. A Pentecostal Apostolic church. I got on my computer and started looking. It was about four in the morning, and I googled Apostolic churches in San Antonio. A picture of a Black couple popped up on my computer screen. The name of the church was Greater Faith Temple Apostolic Church. I printed out the address and decided that I was going to go to church in the morning.

Later that morning, on September 7, 2003, I got in my car and went to church. I sat in the back of this little small church and I don't even remember the message, but I remember the altar call. Before I knew it, I was standing at the altar.

The minister at the altar was Eric Payne. We're still friends to this day. Even though I didn't know him then, I told him how empty I felt. I told him I wanted to be a better man for my sons. He started telling me about Jesus and eventually asked if I had given my life to God. I knew that's what I needed to do. So I was baptized that day and my life changed. For the next eight years, I never missed a service that was held at our new church.

It was an unexpected U-turn that caused me to live, work, and operate in a completely different way.

Digging My Feet
in Sacred Soil

Therefore if anyone is in Christ, he or she is a new creature,
the old things passed away, behold, new things have come.

—2 Corinthians 5:17

I ran home and told my wife, "Look, I've changed."

She was like, "Sure you have. Get out of here with all that."
But I really did feel different, so I begged her to come to the place
that changed me.

"Please just come back to church with me tonight. They
have two services. Let's just take the kids and go back to church."
Eventually, she agreed. So we went back to Greater Faith Temple that
night.

We walked in holding the triplets in their carriers and Ameia in
our arms, and we were rushed by the elderly mothers of the church.
Each grabbing a baby and showering our family with love. Everyone
was just so friendly and so loving. Those people in that small church
became our family. They literally accepted us into their community,
and that gave us a sense of belonging in San Antonio outside of the
military.

Joining that little church when we did was the best thing that
could have happened to our family. Unbeknownst to us at the time,
my wife was pregnant again, and I'm not sure, had there not been
a Godly foundation, what we would have done out of fear. Not too
long after our family joined the Church, our suspicions turned out

to be true. We were definitely about to have another baby, or at least we thought so! We still hadn't shared with anyone the news. What would people say? After all, the triplets had just turned one year old! I was still an airman making only $1,100 a month. What if we had triplets again! These were the thoughts that tormented my mind.

The day finally came for our first ultrasound, we were nervous every day leading up to this day. We actually prayed for God to not give us triplets this time. Well, I'm happy to say, he did answer our prayers. We were not having triplets; however, we were having twins! Unbelievable, right! A single pregnancy, a triplet pregnancy, and now we're having twins.

Surprisingly, there was no fear at the news of our double blessings. I was filled with so much emotion and joy in that moment to know that God favored me so much! I was looking through different lenses this time around. To know that he had confidence in us to gift us with these miracles straight from heaven meant the world to me. Also we were extremely happy that we weren't having triplets again. Twins were a piece of cake compared to triplets. We knew we would be just fine.

On July 3, 2004, my twins Alicia and Naomi made their grand entrance into the world. The most beautiful babies I had ever seen. They were so perfect. No fear at all entered my heart. I was determined to be the best father I could be for all six of my miraculous babies. I thank God for our GFTAC family. They came at the right time and provided the community we were in desperate need of to help raise this quiver full of blessings.

I also met my first mentor around the time the twins were born. His name is Elder Earnest Scott, and he was in charge of all the new converts at GFTAC. The new convert class was his specialty. He just had a beautiful way of dealing with men and women starting their spiritual journey. He knew how to love people beyond their faults and their insecurities. He was the first person in my life who I saw display agape love.

Pastor Douglass Thompson was the senior pastor of Greater Faith Temple, and he later also became a spiritual mentor and father figure in my life. In the early years of my new journey, I called Elder

Scott for everything! I called him for advice. I called him for prayer. I called him as I studied and became a student of the Bible. Elder Earnest Scott was everything this fatherless man ever wanted in a dad. Elder Scott, wanting to honor protocol, began to push me with love toward Pastor Thompson with my questions and need for advice. I wasn't offended because I knew the type of man of honor Elder Scott was. He didn't try to become my pastor, and he wanted me to honor the pastor of the house where God had set me. Looking back, what an honorable thing to do. What a selfless and awesome display of denying one's self and honoring God and the Pastor of the flock of which I was now a member. In Elder Scott, I found relatability, affection, and camaraderie, and it was all instituted by God.

In the twenty-one years that I have known Elder Scott, he has never changed. The love has remained consistent. Even when he needed to discipline and correct me, the love remained the same. God chose Earnest Scott to mentor me in those developmental years as a new believer. The time we spent in prayer and fellowship in the Word, breaking bread often, gave me the confidence to believe in the voice of God in my life. In Pastor Thompson, I found a disciplined life. He taught me to love the Word of God and for it to be the only authority for a believer.

In 2004, I met Tory Smith. He became one of my closest friends and brothers. Watching him accept his call to preach inspired me. I remember going to Pastor Thompson and saying, "I think that I'm a preacher too."

"Well, you need to know for sure, son," Pastor Thomspon said. "I want you to lay before God and allow him to minister to you." So I began to fast and earnestly pray about this call to ministry for about a week before I called Pastor Thompson again.

I called him about 4:00 or 5:00 a.m. "God showed me in a dream how even as a child all I wanted to do was preach. I preached to my sisters and cousins when we played church, studied my pastor at the time, and loved the Bible. God showed me in that dream that I've been a preacher my whole life."

Pastor Thompson concurred and said, "Amen."

So on January 2006, I accepted my call to preach. When I ministered for the first time, I stood in front of a packed church, but I wasn't scared. Something in me knew that I was supposed to be doing this in that moment. I knew that God had my back. I knew for the first time that I was supposed to be helping people believe in and on him that loved all of us before the foundation of the world. I engulfed myself in the gospel message.

I loved seeing people inspired. I loved seeing people changed and motivated. I loved seeing people empowered. Serving in ministry did something to my psyche. My whole life became about helping people improve themselves. God, through Greater Faith Temple Apostolic Church, gave me the right foundation.

I remained at that church for the next thirteen years of my life. During my time there, I learned to serve. I also learned that my words had power and that I was great at public speaking. Those gifts and talents helped catapult me into the next phase of my life and career.

One of very few photos of me in clergy attire.

Min Tory Smith, Min Jamar Dean, and me with our Pastor Bishop Douglass Thompson. We served as adjutants together.

Feeling Myself

Let him who stole steal no longer, but rather let him labor, working with his hands what is good, that he might have something to give to him who has need.

—Ephesians 4:28

After being out of the military for a year, I worked on base as a civilian DOD security officer. I stood at the gate of the base and ushered people through. In order to do the job, I had to get my license to carry weapons as a security guard. On what seemed like an ordinary day, I received a call from a security company based in Grand Rapids, Michigan, named Corporate Security Solutions (CSS). They saw on an old resume of mine on Monster.com that I had a license to carry a weapon for security services, and wanted to know if I wanted to work for FEMA as a contractor. The assignment, which was temporary, could have lasted anywhere from two to thirty weeks. Although the job seemed interesting, I had a good job with benefits on base. The only thing I really needed was more money. My wife and I had six children at the time, and although I was working, we were struggling to make ends meet.

"We're paying two grand a week," the recruiting officer said. I was sold.

"When do I start?" I replied immediately. In my mind, this opportunity came directly from God. Although it was a blessing, the job forced me to sacrifice. I had to live in a hotel in Austin which was about an hour and a half away from my family. But my wife and I agreed that it was worth the sacrifice.

My shift was from 6:00 a.m. to 6:00 p.m. I was so happy to have a job paying that much money. I made sure my uniform had been to the cleaners before my shift and that my shoes were shined. I even showed up at 5:30 a.m. every morning just to be the first person on duty. Every day maybe a few minutes after I arrived, this white gentleman named Tom would also show up at the site. He came in with his coffee and smoked a cigarette. We engaged in a little bit of small talk here and there, but from what I could tell, he was a FEMA contractor like me. Out of sixteen security officers, I was the only one to show up early, so Tom and I built a small, but friendly relationship.

Little did I know that Tom was the Director of FEMA Security. I didn't know it at the time, but Tom emailed the owners of the company I was working for, inquiring about this kid who showed up at 5:30 a.m. every morning. He told them, "If you can get everybody to do what he's doing, you guys will have the FEMA contract even longer."

I received a call from Andy Shaffer, the COO of CSS, and he said, "I hear you're doing a great job out there at the joint field operations for FEMA."

"I'm trying. No one has said anything bad about me."

"Well, you show up every morning at 5:30. Why are you doing that? Your shift doesn't start until 6:00 a.m."

"Could be the military," I responded. "I haven't quite become completely civilianized just yet."

"You know Tom?

"Yeah! He's one of the FEMA workers here. I talk to him every morning."

"No, he's not just a FEMA worker. You've been talking to one of the head guys of FEMA across the nation." I was so shocked. "Whatever you're doing, Sishman, you need to make sure all the rest of the guys are doing it too." Then he told me right then and there that I was in charge. "You're the supervisor now, and I want to give you an extra $500 a week."

I was excited, ecstatic, shocked, grateful, and nervous. I had never been a supervisor, but for me, this was all connected to my faith in God. All of these moments in time I now know for sure were connected.

It seems like the defining moments in my life are all connected somehow, that if one piece was out of place, the others could not happen! Take a look and see how they're connected.

One Saturday night after hitting the bars, I was frustrated and I made up my mind to attend church. That led to my faith in God beginning to grow. I took a risk, quit my job on base, and took a temporary security job with FEMA. I put my best foot forward. Met a guy named Tom. And then I became a supervisor. Every moment I mentioned was predicated on the moment prior to taking place.

I went to the guys I was now over and said, "I don't know what just happened, but they just told me I'm the new supervisor. We've been up here for the last three weeks getting to know each other and having fun. Nothing is going to change. But I want you to represent the company well and represent yourselves well." Since I had already built a healthy relationship with them, they agreed to have my back. I led that operation, and FEMA loved us. My wife and kids came up on the weekends. We had extra money. It was just a beautiful time. About fifteen weeks after I became a supervisor, Andy called me again. He said, "We want to know if you'll come on as a full-time employee with CSS?" As good as the offer sounded, I didn't want to be a private security guard. I was hoping to get my federal security job back on base.

"I'm not asking you to be a guard. We just landed a large contract in San Antonio, and we want you to run the San Antonio operation. Your official title would be general manager. Do you believe you can do this? Do you want the job?"

Without even thinking, I said, "I do." And with that, I flew out to Michigan to the corporate office for training. Being the only Black general manager at CSS made me feel intimidated at first, but eventually, I found my stride.

I grew the San Antonio operation from one contract to twenty-two contracts in eighteen months. San Antonio grew 126 percent in my first eighteen months as general manager. I found my niche, and my confidence grew. Although my salary did not.

Eighteen months after I accepted the general manager position with CSS, my 50k annual salary had not changed. It was nothing to me because I felt indebted to the company for giving me an opportunity. Although confident, I was still ignorant of the value I brought to the team. It took one of my close friends, John Belvin, at dinner one evening to help me realize that. John asked if they were compensating me for the growth of the business. I told him my salary hadn't changed, but I was sure they would review it after a couple of years. John Belvin asked if he could help me prepare a letter asking for an increase in salary. I was terrified because, in my mind, they had given me the opportunity in the first place. I hadn't yet fully realized that I earned it. I was 100 percent certain that as soon as they read my letter, they were going to take the opportunity away from me. Although I had grown and recognized my strengths, I didn't really know who I was and what value I brought to their company.

John helped me write the letter asking for a rate increase, listing all the things I had done. Andy emailed me back immediately and let me know that my new salary was $63,000 annually plus a nice bonus package for future contracts! I went on to make six figures for the first time in my life that year.

I was so happy and relieved that I still had a job. But most of all, I was feeling myself that day. Learned a valuable lesson in business: "closed mouths don't get fed." Sometimes you have to take the lead in negotiating your worth. I was finally living the life that Li'l Man dreamed of, and it felt oh-so good.

My first management position. I was the General
Manager, San Antonio region for CSS, USA.

A Hard, But Necessary Lesson

Many are the plans in the mind of a man, but it
is the purpose of the Lord that will stand.

—Proverbs 19:21

Life was great. I finally found my niche. I fell in love with the security industry, and business was booming! I had become an expert not only in managing operations, but I was a pretty good salesman too.

On one particular Friday, Andy, the COO of CSS showed up at my office. Usually, when I knew he was coming, I would have fruit trays out and make sure the office was in tip-top shape. But he showed up out of the blue, around 4:30 p.m., right before we were about to close.

"Sishman," he said, walking through the door.

"Hey," I said, surprised. "What are you doing here? Happy to see you."

"How are you doing?

"I'm good."

"Can we talk in your office?"

"Sure," I said, inviting him into my office. When he sat down, I didn't get a good vibe about the visit. "What's going on?"

"Well, I have some good news and some bad news. What do you want first?"

"Give me the bad news first."

"As of 5:00 p.m. tonight, we've sold the company." Five o'clock was literally twenty minutes from the moment he walked into my office. But that wasn't necessarily a bad thing. "We sold CSS to US Security, and they didn't pick up your contract."

"So I don't have a job?"

"As of 5:00 p.m. today, no."

"I couldn't get a heads-up."

"Honestly, no. But the good news is all 116 of your employees will be grandfathered over into the new company.

"So everyone has a job except me." I was so hurt. I had to fight back tears. It was such a defining moment in my life and new career. That's when I learned that business is cutthroat. I realized that I needed to look out for myself. Even though I wasn't thinking about owning my own security company at that moment, I later realized that God was pushing me in that direction. "So everything is done, Andy?" I asked.

"We're going to pay you, Sishman. We're going to keep paying you your salary for three months. You did an excellent job. It's not personal, it's just business. But I need your keys and your company credit card."

And just like that, it was over. I didn't have a job. I felt shattered.

I started applying for all these other security jobs, but no one would hire me.

Eventually, I started working for a smaller security company that I hired as a subcontractor for one of my contracts while with CSS. The name of the company was Blue Armor Security Services. It was owned by Willie Ng, a local San Antonio police officer with a great reputation throughout the city. My salary dropped from $63,000 to $50,000 with no bonuses or benefits. This time, I knew my worth and was willing to show the value I would bring to his company first. It was a different opportunity for me because Blue Armor didn't have everything together and organized like CSS. I remained there for the next six years of my life.

In those six years, Blue Armor Security became the largest minority security company in south Texas. I helped make Blue Armor a multimillion-dollar company. One day I arrived in the office early and sat at my desk, and it dawned on me that I was always at Blue Armor Security, and Willie never was. Then I thought about my time at CSS USA. The guys at CSS were never there either. So I started thinking to myself, *Sishman, why can't you do this on your own?* The same answer kept replaying over and over in my mind.

I didn't have the capital. It's a fact: in order to make money, you have to spend money. My mindset was changing, but I stayed with Blue Armor because I needed to take care of my family.

Unfortunately, things with Blue Armor became toxic. The owner brought his wife in to take over the entire operation. I felt restricted and micromanaged in such a way that I felt I was being forced out. Sensing what was coming, I formed my own LLC, eventually ended up quitting Blue Armor Security, and picked up a side hustle with a financial services company named Primerica Financial Services.

I stepped out on faith. I had a plan, but as we all know, things in life sometimes don't go according to our plans.

My wife and I separated. I was alone. Money was tight. Things just weren't coming together like I thought they would.

I had all these hopes and dreams, but in reality, I was about to hit rock bottom.

Hitting Rock Bottom

When you pass through the waters, I will be with you
and when you pass through the rivers, they will not
sweep you. When you walk through the fire, you will
not be burned, the flames will not set you ablaze.

—Isaiah 43:2

As everything seemingly fell apart, my anxiety went through the roof. I stayed by myself in my apartment often. I was struggling financially, and life dealt me a bad hand full of unexpected loss and grief.

In 2015, my grandmother on my dad's side; my auntie Maria on my mom's side, who was like my older sister; and my aunt Carolyn, my dad's only sister, all passed away within months of each other.

My grandmother lived to be ninety-six years old. When God took her, she experienced no pain. The day before she died, she was outside raking her yard. She was full of life and had no chronic pain or issues.

My aunt Maria battled heart problems for a while. She was fifty years old when she passed away. Even though she was young, she lost her battle with heart disease. Since my grandmother helped raise me, my aunties were like my big sisters. So that loss hit hard.

My aunt Carolyn was murdered. She was sixty-two years old when she left this earth. She was mentally disabled. She worked at the same grocery store for thirty-five years. She took the same bus every day and walked home after work. On the day she was murdered, a fifteen-year-old young man beat her to death with a pipe and did gruesome things to her body.

All of this took a toll on me, especially because this was the same year I separated from my ex-wife, and that marriage ended in divorce not long after.

Mentally, I went through a lot that year. That's when I started therapy. I'm a huge promoter of mental health. I think it's a great thing to sit on somebody's couch and unpack everything you've experienced, thought, and felt.

Therapy helped me connect the dots in my life. Therapy also helped me unpack the file cabinets of thoughts and beliefs I had unintentionally stored in the back of my brain. And therapy helped me realize that there's power in confession. That's biblical. Things happen when you open up your mouth and release words from the abundance of your heart. Through the power of faith, therapy, and a desire to become my greatest potential, I started an ongoing habit of positive self-talk. I talk to myself every morning even to this day! I confess every day that "today is the day that my life will be revolutionized by my choices."

I found myself starting to live up to my confession! Seeking to be the best version of myself every day. I learned to confess that *today is the day that my life will be revolutionized by my choices*. I learned to confess over my life that I was going to walk into my greatest potential. Confession is powerful. It heals, and it can actually help shape your destiny.

I have never experienced the death of three loved ones in a year, let alone the death of a marriage. 2015 was the hardest year of my life. I literally hit rock bottom. If it wasn't for therapy, I could have easily become an alcoholic during that season of my life. I had picked up the habit of drinking, and I wasn't my best self at all. What's insane to me was that I found the help I needed at that rock bottom place. Had nowhere else to look, but up!

I was on a steep slope. My only two options were to go six feet under the ground, or I was going to rise up in faith. Figuratively speaking, I was really between life and death at that point. I did what God said in Deuteronomy 30:19. He said, "I have set before you life and death, blessing and curses, therefore choose life that both you and your seed may live." So grateful that at my lowest rock bottom place, I decided to choose life and to get up from where I was and chase after my potential.

My Auntie Ree Ree. My big sister was one of three
family members that passed in 2015.

My dear Aunt Carolyn. She was my dad's only sibling. She
was murdered and snatched away from us in 2015.

I called her "Pretty Lady". This was Grandma Rimpson,
my dad's mom. She lived to see 96 full years of life.

Classes with a Beautiful Lady

The Lord said, "It is not good for man to be alone.
I will make a helper suitable for him."

—Genesis 2:18

After searching high and low for another job, I decided to go back to school since they pay veterans to do so. It was a win-win. More experience and more money.

I distinctly remember trying to focus in one of my classes, but there was a beautiful chocolate lady that kept grabbing my attention. I was sitting right next to her, so I decided to ask her name.

"Britney," she said.

"I'm Sishman." Since we had a class together, we eventually began working on assignments and group projects together. I began to build a friendship with this young lady. She had served in the military like me. She was actually thinking about going back into the military, but I told her about applying for disability as a veteran. I let her know that she could get paid without having to go back into active duty. I helped her with that. In time, we became very good friends. She told me she was a divorced mother of three. We just had a lot in common, and eventually, something happened that I didn't think would happen.

After talking for several months, I started to fall in love with this woman. She was just so selfless, understanding, and kind to me. I told myself I was never getting married again, but my feelings toward her kept growing.

She's tough. She can handle me which not too many people can. She was willing to help me in a moment in my life where my confidence had dwindled down to pretty much nothing. I couldn't find a top-tier job, so I took a job at an entry-level position, making $30,000 a year. But she loved me through all of that. She even helped me out financially.

I talked to my pastor, Bishop Brent Bryant, at my church about Britney, and he encouraged me to bring her to a service. So I did. When she and I made up our mind to allow God into our relationship, that's when we could really see clearly and focus on his will for our lives. We decided during that time to take sex off the table in an effort to focus on growing and connecting emotionally, and both of us submitted to counseling together. So our counseling transitioned into premarital counseling, and we set a date to get married. My pastor was so happy to know that he had a hand in bringing these two families together, Bishop Brent Bryant will forever have a special place in our hearts.

I was so scared about whether or not Britney would connect with my kids and vice versa. That soon became the least of my worries. My kids loved Britney, and her kids loved me. All of us began to spend a lot of time together. We went to church, enjoyed each other's company, and spent a lot of quality time getting to know one another.

Even though we had originally set our wedding date far off, our pastor advised us to have a small ceremony with our closest family and friends. He told us we could plan a larger celebration later for everyone else. We listened to his counsel, and that's exactly what we did.

We sat down and talked to our kids. They were all for it. We sat down and talked to our parents. I met with Britney's biological dad and the man who helped raise her. Both of them gave me their blessing. On November 17, 2017, I married Britney and gained three beautiful bonus babies: Larry, Lakyla, and Terrell.

We started our journey together in a small three-bedroom apartment. Even though in many ways, I still felt like my life was at rock bottom, thanks to my wife's support, I started to feel hope again.

A little less than a year later, in October of 2018, I heard a sermon preached by a guest pastor at our church, Apostle Kevin Duhart. The message was entitled "This Is My Soil." He said if you want to bear fruit, you have to cultivate the land. He said you have to get out there, work, and get your hands dirty. Those words did something to me that day. I thought to myself *how dare I give up on the seed God planted in my heart to be an entrepreneur.*

No one in my family had ever been an entrepreneur. No one in my family owned a business. They worked hard for somebody else. I had a family full of hard workers, but no one was working for their own name. I wanted to be the first to blaze the trail. I told my wife how much that message moved me. At the time, we had $2,000 in the bank. We were saving up for this big wedding, but Britney said, "Take the money and go get all your licenses back." We spent all our money getting those licenses together to get my security company back active and ready for business. I wanted to be prepared when it happened!

Even though we were optimistic about our future, trying to plan this extravagant wedding was getting expensive. We decided to do a destination wedding instead because we could pay for it bit by bit. So we decided to have our larger celebration in Jamaica. Her best friends came. Her cousin, who is like her sister, came, and the man who helped raise Britney came and walked her down the aisle.

During our time in Jamaica, I spent a lot of time before starting our day, just thanking God for a second chance at life, just talking to him in the cool of the day. On our last morning in Jamaica, while in prayer I heard God say to me, "You don't have to strive any longer. Just be still." Those words were like a second wind to me. When we returned home, I stopped worrying about how the business was going to happen. I just started getting up every day to be the best version of myself I could be.

Almost a year later, while at work, I got a call from a guy named Gabe McCain with Atkins Construction.

"Is this the owner of SMR Security?" I almost forgot I changed the name of my company when I reinstated all of the business certifications. Its original name was Whole Armor Security, but after reinstating the business certs, I learned that name had been assumed by some other entity. After a dream one night after praying and stressing about a new name, I saw in my dream the name SMR Security Services! It was surrounded by lights and people clapping. When I woke up, I knew I had my answer.

I thought to myself, *no, I don't want it to be all about me*, because "SMR" are my initials. Then I saw the following words just as clear as day: safety, management, reliability. It was definitely a defining moment.

Okay, back to the phone call. So I'm at work and receive a call.

"Yes, this is Sishman," I replied.

He said, "My company just won a contract with the San Antonio Water System, and they require us to have nineteen-percent minority-owned participation with our construction contract. We're wanting to give some of that to a minority-owned security company. He went on to explain how he found us through our certification with the South Texas Regional Certification Agency, the certification we reactivated after hearing Apostle Duhart's message, "This is My Soil."

"Are you able to do that? I know it's Thanksgiving eve, but can you start tomorrow, Thanksgiving morning?"

I was honest with Gabe. "I don't even have any employees. I literally just started my company back up. I don't even have any money to pay the payroll."

He said, "I need your certifications. So I'm going to ask you one more time. Do you want this contract?"

"Yes."

"Great. What's your billing rate? I know this is short notice, so I know it may be kind of high." I threw out the highest number within reason I could think of. He said, "Write me an invoice for the next two months and come pick up the check tomorrow morning."

With tears in my eyes, I replied, "Yes, sir!"

I knew this defining moment was directly connected to every other defining moment in my life. God was definitely ordering my steps and opening doors I would've never dreamed he'd open.

Suddenly, just like that, my life as I knew it would never be the same. Someone needed the vision of my business before my business really existed. Gabe and Atkins Construction needed the vision to become reality. What if I had not gone to church that Sunday? What if I hadn't heard the message that moved me to get our credentials and certifications active? If I had not done any of those things, I don't know that I'd be writing this book at all. God worked it out so that I didn't need to worry about floating payroll. I didn't need to get a loan. God literally set it up where I went to pick up a check the next morning for $62,000. That was more money than I'd ever seen in my life at that time. SMR Security, the company that I am still the CEO of today, was launched just like that from our three-bedroom apartment, and we haven't looked back since.

Britney and I at our graduation receiving our BAs in Business from the University of Phoenix. What a wonderful day!

My wife and I are both veterans of the United States
Military! Here's a side-by-side of us in our BDUs!

Britney and I in Jamaica at our destination wedding/
honeymoon. We definitely need to go back there soon!

Me and my gorgeous bride in Jamaica on our
wedding day! This is my fav pic of that day.

Brit and Sish, my best friend.

Our actual wedding day. This was a private ceremony with our
children, parents, grandparents, and a few close friends.

Our destination wedding and Britney's favorite picture of us. I love it, too!

A true King and Queen indeed!

Brit and I with our Pastor … (Pops). We love him dearly. He
believed in us and helped us get to where we are today.

Realizing It Ain't All About Me

Do nothing out of selfish ambition or vain conceit.
Rather, in humility, value others above yourself.

—Philippians 2:3

Life was finally on the up and up. The contract with Atkins Construction lasted two years and paid my company close to 300k. Things were going so well with SMR Security that I was able to quit my full-time job and be a full-time entrepreneur. My wife and I turned our White Mitsubishi SUV into a company vehicle, and shortly after that, I won another contract. I started submitting proposals relentlessly, and before I knew it, SMR Security had five contracts.

The days were long, but I was in full-fledged hustle mode. I was literally working eighteen to nineteen hours a day. I was only getting about three hours of sleep because I had to go and work security posts.

I was trying to figure out how to run a business while I was working sixty plus hours a week in the business. I was thrown abruptly into this life of entrepreneurship, but it didn't matter to me if I ever slept. I was built for this. I realized every defining situation in my life led up to this moment. It was almost as if God said *you know how to run a business because I placed you in organizations where you ran other people's businesses. You know how to do payroll. You know how to hire people. You know how to handle client interaction. You know how to talk to a boardroom full of people because I trained you.* I realized that God had set me up for success by ordering my steps. But I needed to be reminded that my success wasn't just for me and mine.

I was in my office one day when I heard a distinct but familiar voice. "I just want to work full-time. I have my license." I couldn't see the person from my office, but I was certain it was Mr. Howard Overstreet, a previous colleague and coworker of mine that I hadn't seen in years. I called out to him from my office.

"Howard?"

"Did someone just call my name?" I walked out toward the lobby area and called out to him. He recognized me immediately. "Sishman Rimpson," he said, his face lighting up a bit. It had been years since we'd seen each other.

Shortly after we hugged and embraced each other, I said, "Man, you don't have to do an interview. You're hired." Howard and I had a long-standing history, and there was no way I was going to let him go without a job.

Howard and I worked together when I was a security guard on Randolph Air Force Base. Even though Howard was a great worker, the supervisor on base mistreated him because he thought he was too old to represent our guard force. Seeing Howard get mistreated made me realize that I had a problem with bad leadership. Whether I meant to be or not, I was always the type of person to help the underdog. Maybe it started because I had to protect my sisters, but I always felt compelled to come to the aid of people who were being mistreated.

The supervisors on base would intentionally try to make Howard fail his mandatory inspections. I stepped in one day and said, "Quit mistreating him." From that moment on, the head supervisor wanted me gone. I risked losing my job taking up for Howard that day, and I'd do it all over again just the same. Eventually, Howard failed his inspection, and he was let go.

So it was easy for me to hire Howard without thinking twice about it. After about six months, Howard showed up at the office and asked my assistant if he could speak to me. I was happy to hear Howard was in the office and went to greet him. I immediately noticed that Howard had lost about fifty pounds. He was in uniform, but it was falling off of him. "What's going on, man?" I said, concerned about him.

"Boss, can we go to your office?"

"Yeah, of course. And quit calling me boss, man." We walked in, and Howard closed the door behind us. We both sat down and I noticed tears begin forming in Howard's eyes.

"I don't know if I can continue working, Sishman. Doctors are telling me I have pancreatic cancer. All my children live out of town and have their own lives. I'm here all by myself. The doctors are telling me I have to go to the hospital. Sishman, you're the only person I could think of to talk to." Then out of the blue, Mr. Overstreet asked me to pray for him. "I came to see you, Sishman, because I wanted to know if you'll pray with me."

At that moment it felt like a brick had hit me in the chest. I had forgotten that my elevation and success weren't about me. It wasn't about money, my briefcase, my big office, or my ego and pride. What if all of my success was for this moment to come about!

We stood up with tears in our eyes. I reached for Howard's hand, but in what seemed to be a moment of desperation, Howard grabbed me and embraced me. My friend, Mr. Overstreet, wept in my arms as I prayed for him. It was a defining moment in my life I'll never forget. It brought me back down from my high place to a place of humility. I asked him if he wanted me to go to the hospital with him. He said no and told me that his daughter was going to be there on the phone with him. He thanked me for the prayer, we embraced, and he went on his way.

A few weeks passed, and I hadn't heard from Howard. I became really nervous because Howard wasn't answering his phone. I called his daughter who was listed as his emergency contact, and she told me he was at the hospital. She also told me that she couldn't make it to the hospital to visit him. So I decided to shut the office down one day, and the office staff and I went and visited Mr. Overstreet. I told his daughter not to tell Howard I was coming because I wanted to keep my visit a surprise.

When we got to the hospital, Howard was looking out the window. He was curled up, pale, and looking like he was about to leave this earth. I said, "Have a good one, Howard," which is a phrase he always used to say hello and goodbye. He turned around and yelled my name.

"Sishman," he exclaimed. It was almost as if life came back into his body. "What are you doing here?"

With tears in my eyes, I said, "I had to come to see about my friend." We stayed there for a couple of hours. We laughed, talked, and just had a good time together. But in my gut, I knew that would be the last time I saw him. I told him how much I loved him and cared for him. I asked if he needed anything. He wanted lunch, so I went and got what he requested and brought it back to him. When we left Howard that day, he was full of life and had the biggest smile on his face.

A week from that day, his daughter called me, letting me know that Mr. Overstreet died. She then said, "Mr. Rimpson, I don't know what you did to my daddy, but he loved you. He always talked about you."

Talk about a defining moment! This man literally helped me remember there's a God behind the scenes working out his will through our everyday lives and choices. I'm just so grateful he thought enough of me to allow my path to cross with Mr. Howard Overstreet.

I haven't operated the same since. I've come to realize that my life, my work, success, and achievements aren't all about me at all. Life is best spent when you can find purpose in whatever it is that you do. I reconnected with purpose on that day Mr. Howard Overstreet walked into my office.

My friend, Mr. Howard Overstreet. One of the
nicest, kindest men I've ever met in my life.

A Divine Meeting with "Nate the Great"

For I know the plans I have for you, declares the
Lord, plans to prosper you and not to harm you,
plans to give you a hope and a future.

—Jeremiah 29:11

Thinking about the loss of Howard makes me think about my own family. I didn't have a traditional upbringing. My life didn't always go as planned. But God has made everything right. My mom is celebrating twenty years of sobriety. Looking at her now, there's no hint that she ever was even addicted to drugs. Although my father spent two decades of his life in prison, before he left this earth, he would become my best friend.

I was twenty-nine or thirty years old when my dad got out of prison. It had been twenty-two years since I last saw him. I was so excited to see my daddy again.

Without even thinking twice about it, I called my dad who was staying with my grandma and let him know when I was coming home to Gary to see him. I made sure he knew the dates and the time I would be there. I didn't want anything to take away from this moment. So many thoughts ran through my mind on the plane ride from San Antonio to Gary. Would he like me? Would he be proud of me for being in the military? Would he be standoffish? My brain couldn't rest.

The plane landed, and I got my rental car and headed to see my daddy. Couldn't believe this was really happening. I pulled up to my grandmother's house nervous about whether or not I was enough for my pops. I wasn't a gangster like him and my older brother Nate. I chose another route. Sitting in that car, I took one last deep breath and got out of the car and knocked on the door. As always, my beautiful grandmother came to the door, smiling from ear to ear, screaming, "Li'l man is here!"

I embraced my grandmother and my aunt Carolyn as I was looking and waiting for my daddy to come from that back room, but he didn't come.

I asked where my daddy was, and my grandmother said, "He's coming, baby, he'll be here any minute." So I sat there with my grandma, waiting. An hour passed. Two hours passed. Then three hours passed. At this point, my grandma started to get mad.

"Where is your no-good daddy? He knows you came here to see him."

I just smiled and said, "It's okay, Grandma." Five hours passed. Then six hours passed. My biggest fear had become true: my daddy didn't want anything to do with me. I tried my best to not show the disappointment on my face, but I was crushed.

I felt so small. It was hard because I was so excited to see him, but why wasn't he excited to see me? I only flew in for the night and was scheduled to leave first thing in the morning to head back to Texas. After waiting for hours upon hours. I hugged and kissed my grandmother and auntie Carolyn and told them I would try again in a couple of months when I could save up more money for a flight. I left my grandmother's house that night feeling rejected by my dad for the first time in my life. I was hurt, but God had a plan.

I called my aunties, who are like my sisters, and I told them I wanted to go out to eat to take my mind off everything. They told me about a restaurant we could go to. So my aunts took me out. We ate and had a good time, but my thoughts started to get me down. *Maybe he doesn't know how to be a dad. Maybe he doesn't want to be one.*

So while we were at the restaurant, I noticed this man with dreadlocks sitting afar off at another table. I didn't know a lot about my dad, but I knew he had dreadlocks, but his back was all we could see. Throughout the whole night, I'm staring at this man. He had a suit on. My dad wore suits all the time. Pimp-like suits with socks that look like stockings. I'm there, but my mind is focused on this man whom I know can't be my daddy! It's impossible, right? How would we end up at the same exact restaurant without each other knowing we'd be there? I'll tell you why, because there's a God always working behind the scenes of our lives!

The man stuck his leg out from underneath the table, and I'll be—he had those stocking-like socks on! My aunt Cat was like, "What are you looking at?" after watching me stare at this dude for about an hour. Even though his back was facing me the entire time, I got enough nerve to get up and approach him. I said to my aunt Cat,

"Auntie, is that my daddy?"

"Boy, where?" She looked and said, "Naw, that ain't him." But I got up anyway and walked to the table.

"Daddy?" He turned around, and to my surprise, it was indeed my daddy! Goosebumps, right? You can't tell me that God isn't real!

He jumped up, literally picked me up, and even though I was thirty years old, I instantly became a child again. "My baby," he said, kissing me like I was a baby. He picked me up again and hugged me. The whole restaurant started clapping. I just couldn't believe it!

It was one of the greatest moments of my life. Even though I was grown and had big muscles, at that moment, I was that eight-year-old boy that said goodbye to his daddy twenty-two years prior. That embrace meant everything to me. He held me for what seemed like fifteen minutes. We went over to the table, and he saw my aunties for the first time in twenty years. There was just so much love in that moment. I spent the entire night with him. We laughed and talked literally all night long, and I flew back to San Antonio the next morning.

I realized that I had tried to make every man that had come into my life a dad figure. It took that moment to make me realize that I only had one Daddy. I tried to make all these other men in my life—coaches and pastors—my father, but I would always end up disappointed because the expectation I placed on them could never be accomplished. They couldn't fulfill the longing I had to know my daddy. But God knew, and he had a plan.

His plan was to answer the prayer of that eight-year-old boy in me that longed to have his daddy in his life. God did it, and as always, he made the moment a defining moment for me! For the time I had left with my dad, fatherhood was redeemed, and I gained a relationship with the most impactful man I'd ever come to know, my daddy.

Me and the old man on one of my trips to Gary to spend time with him.

Redeeming Fatherhood

Yet God has made everything beautiful in its own time. He has planted eternity in the human heart, but even so, people cannot see the whole scope of God's work from beginning to end.

—Ecclesiastes 3:11 New Living Translation

After being reunited with my dad, I flew home about fifty to sixty times to spend time with him over the years. We did whatever we could to make up for the time we didn't have together.

When my grandma died, we got even closer. He cried like a baby, and I had never seen him emotional like that. He called me when she was dying. I was in Texas, and he was in Gary. He couldn't give the doctors the order to unplug the machine, even though Grandma had been brain-dead for over an hour.

"I can't do it," he admitted to me over the phone. So I walked him through the process, let him take as long as he needed to make peace with Grandma leaving this world. When he was at peace, he gave the doctor the okay, and Grandma passed within minutes afterward. That level of vulnerability did something to me and my daddy. It took our relationship to another level. While I was there with him at the funeral, I noticed that he wasn't drinking, which was odd. My dad was an alcoholic, so when I saw that he wasn't drinking, I said, "What's wrong with you?"

"My stomach has been hurting. I don't know what's going on with my stomach." We didn't know it at the time, but my dad had pancreatic cancer.

Over the next year, my dad started having problems using the restroom. He had difficulty controlling himself. I flew home to take him to the doctor. When I got there, I was blown away. Only a year had passed since my grandmother's funeral, but my dad has lost an extreme amount of weight. He was getting smaller and smaller. Eventually, he had to stop working.

At first, the doctors said it was irritable bowel syndrome. But it wasn't. Eight years after being reunited with my dad, he was diagnosed with pancreatic cancer. I'll never forget the day the doctor told my dad that the cancer was terminal.

The doctor said, "Mr. Rimpson, the cancer has spread and progressed throughout your body. Unfortunately, there is nothing we can do, as the cancer is terminal." I asked the doctor how much time my dad had left, but my dad didn't want to know.

My dad said, "Son, you can talk to him? I want you to know, but don't tell me." So we stepped out of the office. The doctor told me my dad had eleven months to live, but he only lived for six.

After that appointment, my dad's and my relationship changed because he was dying. My dad's close friends remained there and were loyal to my father until the day he died. He was far from the "Nate the Great" everyone once knew. He wasn't the gangster that threw crazy parties anymore. During his last few months, our relationship gained so much substance and depth, and I was blessed to be with my dad up until his dying day.

Although the time we had together was short, we redeemed it. Despite such a rocky and uncertain start, my dad became my very best friend. Despite being a gangster and a street dude, my dad died an honorable man.

I gave the eulogy at my dad's funeral. The message was entitled, "Honor Thy Father." I told our story to those in attendance. I talked about how Exodus 20:12 doesn't say honor your father if he is a good person, or if he's who you want him to be. There's no prerequisite for that honor. I also talked about how when I started selling life insurance as a side hustle, my dad wanted to be one of my first clients to sign up for a life insurance policy. He just wanted to support his baby boy.

He was so excited to get a policy. At the time, he was healthy. We didn't know anything was wrong. So when my dad died, I used some of the insurance money from his policy to start SMR Security Services. To me, that was legacy.

In my daddy's death, he exemplified Proverbs 13:22 which says that "a good man leaves an inheritance for his children's children." So yes, according to that scripture my dad died a good and honorable man.

Fatherhood isn't about being perfect. It's about how you finish, not how you start. Everybody is on a journey to become the best version of themselves.

I thank God for allowing me to get to know my father. My dad's memory lives within me every day. I still honor my father and think about him every day. On his birthday since his death, I dress in a suit like my pops and celebrate the man we called "Nate the Great."

Me, my mom, and dad. They remained friends until
my dad's last breath. Love my parents.

My favorite pic of me and my dad. I love the way he's looking
at me in this pic. His expression is so full of love.

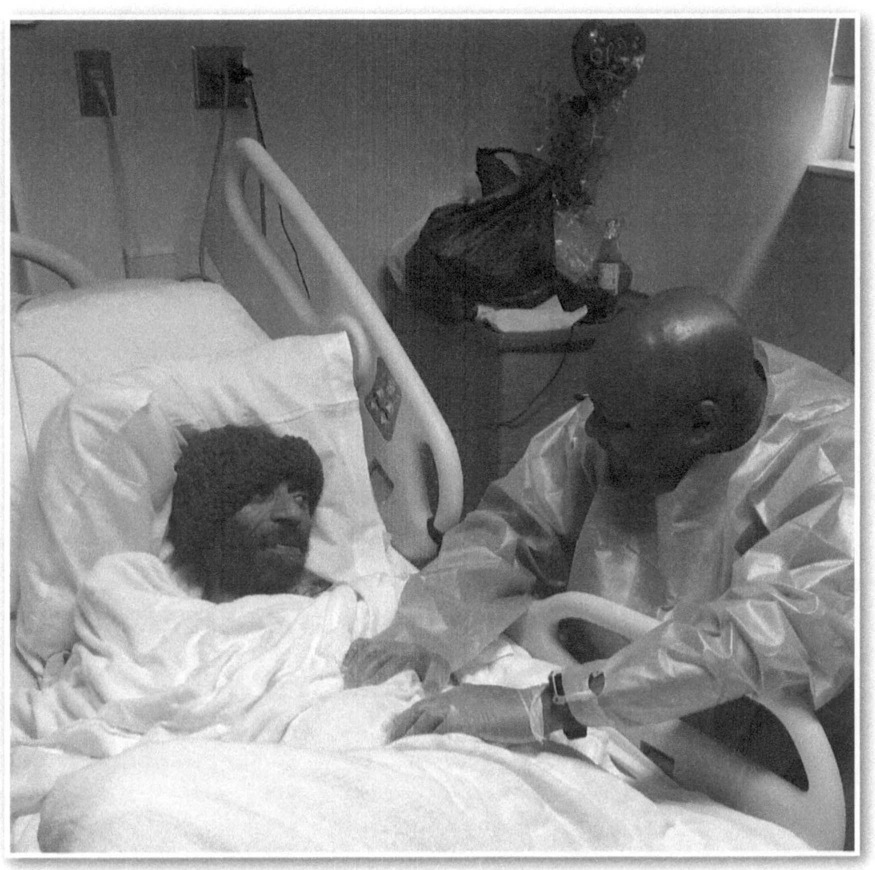

My dad on his death bed. These moments were so precious
between he and I. Sometimes we just stared and cried together.

My dad and I at the funeral of my Auntie Carolyn.
As grown as I was, I was still his baby boy.

My dad and I attending a funeral together. He was getting sicker
by the day but was determined to stay dressed to a tee.

My dad and Brit. He loved Brit as if she were his own, and she
absolutely adored him, too. So glad she got to know him.

A Life-Changing Revelation

Ephesians 1:18 *I pray that God will open your minds to see his truth. Then you will know the hope that He chose us to have. You will know that the blessings God has promised his holy people are rich and glorious.*

As I look back over my life, I realize that a lot of the things I thought mattered didn't.

It didn't matter that I was born and raised in the murder capital of the nation.

It didn't matter that life dealt me some rough and straight-up ugly cards to deal with. The circumstances I was born into—addiction, violence, and poverty—also didn't matter.

What matters is that there is a God who's working behind the scenes in all of our lives, who is going before us in time and making simple ordinary moments, defining moments that change the course of not only our lives but those in our sphere of influence as well.

My life was not about what others before me did, but about what I was willing to do. My choices in life defined me. How I responded to what life dealt defined me! How you respond and what mental notes you take while going through this life have defined you as well. Pay attention to the moments in your own life that helped push you toward your best potential. They might not have been pretty, but they were purposeful. That's what matters.

I strongly believe that nothing happens to us by chance. God has a way of bringing out the best in us by allowing us to overcome challenges. All the pain, fear, rejection, misunderstandings, abandonment, good times, and bad times we experience serve a purpose in our lives. We would never know that we were survivors if we didn't survive the trials that were meant to defeat us.

Going through some of my defining moments didn't feel good at the time, but I am a better man, husband, father, leader, advocate, believer, and person because of the good, bad, and sometimes ugly moments that happened in my life. I realize now that those moments made me who I am today.

You may not realize the defining moments in your life until after you've experienced them. It may be years later when you kick open the back door of your life and realize the moments that led you to become the person you are. That's okay.

I've come to realize that God can use anything. As a matter of fact, He promises to use the good, bad, and ugly moments of life for a greater purpose. Romans 8:28 says: "And we know that all things work together for good for them who love God and are the called according to His purpose." I realize now that the defining moments in my life are included in the "all things" the Bible talks about. This means that everything we go through can work together for good.

Hard times and traumatic moments help drive us deeper into our purpose. Losing my father to years in prison made spending time with him later in life so much sweeter. Growing up around drugs and addiction helped give me a protective spirit. Being poor gave me the drive to work hard and give back to my community. Hitting rock bottom taught me how to take better care of my mental health.

Life won't always feel good, but you've got to take the bruises. You've got to take the stuff that you didn't ask for—like the generational curses—and flip the script. Oftentimes, that's where you'll find your purpose.

I hope this book encourages you to focus on the defining moments in your life and ask yourself: *what are these defining moments meant for? What is the potential of these defining moments? What were those moments meant to cultivate, create, and develop in me?*

I am praying that my story inspires you to serve others, help others, and protect others. Those actions define us.

I hope that these small snippets of defining moments from my life encourage you to look in the mirror and see a champion looking back at you, full of purpose and perseverance. I'm praying that you'll start to see the meaning behind the good, bad, and ugly moments in your life.

Until we meet again, keep going. Chase after the best potential version of yourself. The world needs what you have to offer.

The Rimpson Bunch!

When I met Brit, I didn't know I would inherit three of the
greatest gifts I've ever received! Larry, Lakyla, and Rell

Love this pic of me and my sons! Photo
inspired by my dad, Nate the Great!

A Rimpson night out at the movies!

On March 9th, 2021, our lives got a little sweeter!
Hazel Lynne Rimpson was born!

Daddy's Baby Girl in her SMR Security Onesie!

I truly am a BLESSED MAN!!!

Look up overcomer in the dictionary and you'll see my mama's
pic right there!! No stronger woman on earth! Love you Ma!

Brit and my Mother in Love before church. Love you YaYa.

Thank-Yous for Defining Moments

First, I would like to thank and give honor to the only all-knowing God! The author and finisher of my faith. The orchestrator behind every defining moment in my life! I owe all of the glory to God and him alone!

To my wife, my rock, and my best friend… I am so eternally grateful to be on this journey with you! I am a better man all around because of the woman God has ordained to be my side. I love you, Brit!

To my children, my greatest inspiration to win in life! I love all ten of you more than words can say! It is the absolute honor of my life being your father! There has been no greater joy for me! Thank you!

To my mama, I'm just so proud to be your son! Making you proud of me has become something I long to see on your face! I want you to know that you raised a *good man*, Mama! I've learned how to survive from you! I've learned how not to stay knocked down from my mama, and I'm so grateful for your strength. I love you, Mama.

To my three baby sisters and five older sisters (my aunties), I love you each with my whole heart. To my baby sisters, please know that your brother *adores* each of you! I'm your *only* big brother, and don't ever forget it! To my big sisters, I will forever be your li'l man. Thank you for your consistent unconditional love; it means the world to me!

To my uncles, Reggie, Melvin, Jesse, George, Melvin D, Mark and Dre, and my Auntie Claw, I love you all so much, My uncles, you are the men that stepped in and helped li'l man become a man!

A special *I love you* to my Uncle Reggie and Uncle Melvin and Aunt Claw for being so much more than uncles and an auntie to me! Thank you! To George, Dre, and Mel, I don't know what I'd do if Li'l man didn't have yaw in his life growing up. I love you all!

To all my extended family and friends, I love you.

To my pastors and spiritual mentors over the years, Elder Earnest Scott, Pastor Douglass Thompson, Bishop Brent Bryant, and Apostle Kevin Duhart, I thank God for each of you saying yes to the call of God on your lives. In ways each of you probably don't understand, you've made a permanent *Godly* impact in my life. Thank you so much from the bottom of my heart. I love each of you!

To my best friends and brothers, you know who you are! Day ones and beyond! I'm a blessed man to have each of you brothers in my life! Not every day do family members and friends become closer than *brothers*! We have, and I'm grateful for each and every one of you!

To my daddy, even though you are not here anymore, I feel your presence in every ounce of my being… I am so honored to be "Nate's baby boy." I wear our name "Rimpson" like a badge of honor, Daddy! I thank God every day for making me the son of "Nate the Great." Continue to rest in peace.

To my brother Nate, I love you to *life*, man! So grateful for our bond and our relationship. Your love is so pure, big bro, and I'm so glad that you're in my life. Love you, man!

Lastly, I want to thank all of you for supporting me through the years! My social media family, extended fam, and friends who have *always* supported anything I've ever done, I can't say this enough: *thank you! thank you! thank you!*

I'm sure I forgot someone. Please don't charge it to my heart. I love you all.

Yours Truly,
Sishman

About the Author

Sishman Rimpson is a serial entrepreneur who runs a multimillion-dollar corporation. Together, he and his wife Britney run their businesses and are active parents in the life of their ten children. Sishman graduated with a degree in business and is proud to be a blessing to his community by providing employment opportunities to hundreds of men and women in San Antonio, Texas. In his free time, Sishman's passion is to mentor aspiring entrepreneurs and to encourage people that were born in similar situations and circumstances as he was that the sky is still the limit, and you can do and be whatever you believe you can be! He loves traveling with his family, playing golf, and relaxing at home with family and friends.